# Red
## The Making of Barack Hussein Obama and the Transformation of America

## By Cliff Kincaid

© 2017 by America's Survival, Inc. All rights are reserved worldwide. No part of this document may be reproduced, stored in a retrieval system or transmitted in any form or by any means – electronic, or otherwise, without the prior written permission of America's Survival, Inc.

America's Survival, Inc.
Cliff Kincaid, President
P.O. Box 146, Owings, MD 20736

www.usasurvival.org   443-964-8208

## America's Survival, Inc.

America's Survival, Inc. (ASI) is a leading authority on anti-American extremism, having exposed America's first Marxist president through such blockbuster videos on YouTube and Roku as "The Unvetted," "Marxist Mole: The Story They Can't Kill" and "Obama Admits Communist 'Schooled' Him on White Racism." ASI also exposed America's first openly Marxist big city mayor, Bill "Red Bill" de Blasio of New York City, by releasing an 84-page dossier and a series of videos on his extremist connections. ASI is now a source of information about subversive, radical Islamist, and communist groups advertising themselves as the "resistance" to President Donald J. Trump.

ASI's global Internet-based Roku TV channel, produced in association with broadcaster Jerry Kenney, has over 67,000 total subscribers in more than 60 countries. ASI offers a free mobile device app for Android and iPhones to access our videos, news, and Facebook and Twitter feeds.

ASI websites include:

>   www.usasurvival.org
>   www.noglobaltaxes.org
>   www.religiousleftexposed.com
>   www.sorosfiles.com
>   www.leninandsharia.com

## Cliff Kincaid Bio

America's Survival, Inc. (ASI) President **Cliff Kincaid** is a veteran journalist and media critic who concentrated in journalism and communications at the University of Toledo, where he graduated with a Bachelor of Arts degree. At his college newspaper, Cliff won an award for editorial writing from the Society of Professional Journalists and came to Washington through a national journalism program headed by conservative author and journalist M. Stanton Evans. Hired by Accuracy in Media (AIM) founder Reed Irvine out of college, Cliff served as editor of the AIM Report and director of the Accuracy in Media Center for Investigative Reporting. Cliff served on the staff of *Human Events* for several years and was an editorial writer and newsletter editor for former National Security Council staffer Oliver North at his Freedom Alliance educational foundation.

Cliff is known as an advocate on behalf of the families of victims of terrorism, including the families of victims of the Pan Am 103 bombing. He launched the project on "Justice for Victims of Weather Underground Terrorism" to emphasize the need for action on cold cases involving communist terrorist violence, such as the 1970 bombing murder of San Francisco Police Sergeant Brian V. McDonnell. Cliff also hosted a conference on Puerto Rican FALN terrorism with Joe Connor, whose father was murdered by the FALN, and Richard "Rick" Hahn, a retired FBI agent who specialized in investigations of domestic and international terrorist organizations. Cliff is the author or co-author of several books, including:

- *The Death of Talk Radio?*
- *Why You Can't Trust the News*
- *The Playboy Foundation*
- *Profiles of Deception*
- *The News Manipulators*
- *Global Bondage: The U.N. Plan to Rule the World*
- *Global Taxes for World Government*
- *Blood on His Hands: The True Story of Edward Snowden*
- *Back from the Dead: The Return of the Evil Empire*
- *Red Jihad: Moscow's Final Solution for America and Israel*
- *The Sword of Revolution and the Communist Apocalypse*
- *Marxist Madrassas*
- *Comrade Obama Unmasked: Marxist Mole in the White House.*

What viewers are saying about America's Survival TV on YouTube and Roku:

- Wow. I've just discovered this channel. Thank you! I happened to find America's Survival, Inc. being broadcast on Roku. I am extremely impressed.
- Cliff Kincaid is a true investigative journalist. His articles and videos are always vital and hard-hitting and I always learn something I didn't know before.
- Hi Cliff, love your work on America's Survival! I am from Portugal, but I follow closely what's happening.

**By Cliff Kincaid**

In the year 2017, on the 100th anniversary of the Russian Communist revolution, millions of Catholics and non-Catholics alike are contemplating historical events based on a prophecy. The first appearance or apparition of "Our Lady of Fatima" took place in Portugal on May 13, 1917. The "Miracle of the Sun" on October 13, 1917, which authenticated the vision of three young people, was witnessed by 70,000 people.

Its significance for the secular world consists of an ominous message that Russia would "spread her errors throughout the world, causing wars and persecutions of the Church," if Russia were not converted to Christ. Today, a nuclear-armed and more aggressive Russia still figures prominently in world events, as some Catholic scholars contend the Virgin Mary's request for the consecration of Russia has still not been fulfilled.[1] As a result, the promised "period of peace" was not granted and another world war is possible.

In this prophetic context, Dr. Paul Kengor's new book, *A Pope and a President: John Paul II, Ronald Reagan, and the Extraordinary Untold Story of the 20th Century*, confirms another horrendous crime of the communists -- that the Soviets were behind the May 13, 1981, attempted assassination of Pope John Paul II. The anti-communist pope was a great devotee of Our Lady of Fatima.[2]

Equally significant, the Kengor book looks at President Ronald Reagan's "very deep interest" in Catholicism and the role of Mary, the Mother of God, in human history. [3]

But the Vatican has taken a strange turn, at odds with the anti-communism of Pope John Paul II, sympathetic to the Obama presidency, and now functioning as an integral part of the international Left. The "liberation theology" movement and the reverence for the "Spirit of Gaia" or "Mother Earth" in the name of environmentalism have now assumed prominence under Francis, the first Jesuit pope.

Equally significant, the Vatican is working with the Russian Orthodox Church dominated by Russian President and former Soviet KGB colonel Vladimir Putin, and is defending Islam as a peaceful religion. [4]

Whatever the spiritual nature of the crisis, a politicized Russia-gate investigation threatens the Donald J. Trump presidency while the real Russian agent, former President Obama, is emerging as the Democratic Party's best "weapon" for 2018. [5]

Ominously, on the streets of various American cities, a violent Marxist-oriented Antifa or "anti-fascist" movement has emerged, sometimes in opposition to neo-Nazi or National Socialist organizations.

In regard to this alleged "left-right" confrontation, however, George Watson's profound and important book, *The Lost Literature of Socialism,* reminds us that Adolf Hitler privately "acknowledged his profound debt to the Marxian tradition" and stated explicitly that "I have learned a great deal from Marxism…"

The Nazi regime was destroyed in World War II. But Alex Newman, a contributor to our book *Comrade Obama Unmasked*, noted during an interview on America's Survival TV that "There are actually more people today under communist slavery than there were at the end of the Cold War."

While one estimate of those imprisoned or killed in Hitler's "final solution," the Holocaust, is as high as 20 million lives, the *Black Book of Communism* estimates that the communists have killed as many as 100 million people. And they're not done yet. [6]

In order to understand the global threat, we must confront the nature of the Obama regime and its impact on the Intelligence Community, which has repeatedly failed the American people. Truly understanding the forces behind Obama may help determine who or what is ultimately behind Russia-gate and whether Soviet-style communism really collapsed or just changed its name and form.

The chaos, conflict, and threats include:

- A Chinese Communist- and Russian-backed North Korean regime improving its nuclear weapons capable of hitting the U.S.
- The rise of Russian client state and potential nuclear-armed Iran in the Middle East.

- Reports of Russian arms shipments, some through Iran, to the Taliban in Afghanistan.
- The establishment of a communist dictatorship and civil war in Venezuela.

In an astonishing disclosure about a major crisis close to home, President Trump's CIA Director Mike Pompeo said on the August 13, 2017, edition of "Fox News Sunday" in regard to Venezuela that "The Cubans are there; the Russians are there, the Iranians, Hezbollah are there. This is something that has a risk of getting to a very, very bad place, so America needs to take this very seriously."

Veteran journalist Martin Arostegui, a contributor to our book, *Comrade Obama Unmasked,* blames the crisis in Venezuela on "two decades of U.S. intelligence failures, complacent policies, official negligence and wrongful analysis sometimes planted by Cuban moles in American spy agencies..."[7] The term "moles" means foreign agents or spies.

Since Obama's Secretary of State John Kerry declared in 2013 that the Monroe Doctrine was dead ("The era of the Monroe Doctrine is over."), Venezuela has deteriorated, Putin has traveled to Brazil, Argentina, Nicaragua and Cuba, and Russia has taken control of Venezuela's key oil assets.

Meanwhile, a real and present danger exists of a nuclear attack on America.

"We can't [assume] that having 1,550 deployed strategic nuclear weapons under the New START Treaty somehow deters all our adversaries. It doesn't," said the commander of U.S. Strategic Command, Air Force General John E. Hyten. [8] Unlike in past decades, he said, the 21st century presents more than one adversary and more than one domain. "It's now a multipolar problem with many nations that have nuclear weapons...and it's also multi-domain...We have adversaries that are looking at integrating nuclear, conventional, space and cyber, all as part of a strategic deterrent. We have to think about strategic deterrence in the same way."

The crisis is more dangerous than during the Cold War, when Cuba hosted Soviet nuclear missiles targeting the U.S., and the Castro regime sponsored terrorism on American soil carried out by such groups as the Weather Underground and the Puerto Rican FALN.

Our enemies are outspoken. "Who said communism died?" proclaimed a comic book for children issued by the communist FARC (Revolutionary Armed Forces of Colombia). The book showed Uncle Sam being attacked with the hammer and sickle. [9] In *Comrade Obama Unmasked*, Martin Arostegui examined the report of a link between the FARC narco-terrorists and Obama and his comrades. It was never investigated by the liberal media or Congress.

America has not yet begun to grasp the sinister nature and impact of the Obama presidency. This book attempts to set the record straight.

Simply put, the record shows that President Obama is a Marxist revolutionary and the real Russian agent. As the subtitle of our last book says, he was a Marxist mole in the White House. This isn't just our opinion; communist writer Frank Chapman described Obama's political success as a "dialectical leap ushering in a qualitatively new era of struggle," and quoted Karl Marx, the father of communism, as talking about how "revolutionary struggle" is carried forward by the "mole."

Those who follow America's Survival, Inc. know that we have been warning about Russia long before liberal Democrats began sounding the alarm about alleged Russian connections to the Republican campaign and presidential administration of Donald J. Trump. Our 2014 book, *Back from the Dead: The Return of the Evil Empire,* exposes how America's political leaders and intelligence agencies were caught off-guard as Vladimir Putin brought back the USSR, invaded Ukraine, and now threatens the world with a conflict that could go nuclear. (The book also looked at Russian ties to such figures as former American Ku Klux Klan leader and neo-Nazi David Duke).

Our 2012 conference on Lenin and Sharia represented the first comprehensive effort to link Russia and global communism to global Islam. The conference website, LeninandSharia.com, remains the most authoritative source of information and documents on the Communist-Muslim connection.

Obama, with demonstrable Marxist and Muslim sympathies, is out of office, but his influence is growing, primarily through his Obama Foundation.

In *Comrade Obama Unmasked,* James Simpson examined the Obama Foundation. Its recent statement of donors of over $1 million included:

- Ann & John Doerr
- Exelon Corporation
- Hutchins Family Foundation
- Microsoft Corporation
- New York Community Trust
- Cari & Michael J. Sacks
- Beth and David Shaw
- Michelle Yee & Reid Hoffman

The website declares: "The Obama Foundation will focus on developing the next generation of citizens -- and what it means to be a good citizen in the 21$^{st}$ century."

After leaving the presidency, Obama appeared in Germany and joined with Chancellor Angela Merkel, a former communist youth activist in East Germany, and met with various "young leaders," saying:

> My focus over the next several years, trying to create a network so that we can train the next generation of leaders and that I can help young people like this who are already doing amazing things to get to know each other, across

countries, within countries, [is] to give them the skills and the tools so that they can make even more changes in the future.

We can anticipate how these "changes" are designed to play out.

Young people trained in the "skills" of Saul Alinskyian thought, like Obama, become confused about moral issues and problems. They think, for example, that opposition to the death penalty is on the same moral plane as opposition to abortion, even though traditional religious and moral teaching has never precluded capital punishment. They believe that fighting "global warming" is as important as saving the lives of unborn children or preventing the killing of the elderly. They are trained to fight for homosexual "rights" in violation of traditional religious and moral teaching. They think white supremacy based on race is somehow more abhorrent than Marxist agitation based on class or economic differences. They oppose national sovereignty in favor of open borders and multiculturalism.

As a result of his continuing and even expanding influence, we have taken the time to read and investigate the information in David J. Garrow's 1460-page tome, *Rising Star: The Making of Barack Obama.* In this endeavor, I obtained the assistance of Dr. Tina Trent, who received a degree in British and American Poetry from New College in Sarasota and a doctorate from the Institute for Women's Studies of Emory University, where she wrote about the impact of social movements and popular culture on criminal law under the tutelage of conservative, pro-life scholar Elizabeth Fox-Genovese.

Dr. Trent helped the late Larry Grathwohl release a new edition of his 1976 memoir, *Bringing Down America: An FBI Informer with the Weathermen*, an account of his time infiltrating the Weather Underground. She notes that Garrow won the 1987 Pulitzer Prize in Biography for *Bearing the Cross: Martin Luther King Jr. and the Southern Christian Leadership Conference.* His 1981 book *The FBI and Martin Luther King, Jr.* included an honest discussion of the communist associates of and influence on the civil rights leader.

In the case of documenting Obama's rise to power, Garrow is a man of the left writing about another man of the left. He started conducting what would eventually grow to more than 1,000 interviews over nine years in writing a biography on Obama's life.

However, Garrow's book on Obama is like a 1,000-piece puzzle that, even when assembled, offers no big picture. That is why we have called this particular critique *Red Star Rising.* The red star of communism is what distinguishes Obama. It's what Garrow refuses or fails to grasp in a comprehensive way.

Trent's conclusion, which we share, is that Obama was imposing a deeply Marxist agenda throughout his presidency, from encouraging violent protests against police at home to repositioning foreign policy to reflect leftists' inherent anti-Americanism abroad. She also believes that Obama turned away from working on a legislative approach in order to focus on a Marxist cultural agenda. She says, "Consciously choosing cultural transformation over legislative action as a political strategy would be in character for Obama, given his resistance to working with congressional Republicans, his training as an organizer, and his immersion in identity politics, which was growing into a true religion and obsession of the Left concurrent with his rise to power."

She emphasized the role Obama played in steering social movements from the bully pulpit of the presidency. "Under Obama's watch," she says, "an activist Left was rejuvenated, with the identity politics movement, 'alternative gender' activism, Black Lives Matter, and the culture of continual protest on college campuses growing and engulfing public life."

As a Marxist who actually studied Marxism, Obama was skilled in the "science" of dialectics. In our 2015 book, *The Sword of Revolution and the Communist Apocalypse,* we explore how this strategy is used by the communists on a global basis to confuse the West.

Domestically, Obama was a Marxist specialist in accelerating divisions and conflicts in society. This approach goes far beyond organizing people to polarizing society along racial and other lines.

Our book *Marxist Madrassas* shows how higher education is producing alienated young people with massive student debt and useless degrees, and who are susceptible to Marxism.

Despite the "collapse" of the Soviet Union, the communists reorganized, with dozens of groups active on college campuses and in society at large.

One of them established an alternative to the Communist Party USA called the Committees of Correspondence for Democracy and Socialism (CCDS). Not as widely known, however, is the fact that a secret member of this group was Barbara Lee, who would become a Democratic member of the U.S. Congress, leader of the Congressional Progressive Caucus, and leader of the Congressional Black Caucus.

The 18th International Meeting of Communist and Workers' Parties, was held October 28-30, 2016, in Hanoi, Vietnam. The list of more than 50 communist and "workers" parties in attendance included the Communist Party of China, the Communist Party of the Russian Federation, the South African Communist Party, the Communist Party of Cuba, the Workers Party of [North] Korea, and the Communist Party USA.

CPUSA National Board member Shelby Richardson said, "Many social advances have been won in my country as shown with the election twice of an African American man, Barack Obama as president."[10] Richardson is from Obama's home state of Illinois.

Just days before the 2016 presidential election, Richardson said, "The Communist Party calls for a unity vote to elect [Hillary] Clinton and not risk the danger of a Republican Party victory." Richardson said the Communist Party "must go all out to defeat Donald Trump…"

With the defeat of Clinton and the election of President Trump, the CPUSA is now demanding his impeachment and "expressing outrage over the acts of domestic terrorism carried out by white supremacists, neo-Nazis and fascists in Charlottesville" in Virginia in August.

In the violence which occurred in Charlottesville, Marxist-oriented groups confronted white power groups which had legally obtained a permit to assemble in protest of the removal of a statue of Confederate General Robert E. Lee.

The "Unite the Right" protest in Charlottesville was described as the largest white nationalist rally in the United States in more than a decade. Yet, the neo-Nazi turnout was estimated only in the hundreds while the Antifa "counter-protesters" have appeared in many cities and number in the thousands.

**Agents Provocateurs and Outside Agitators**

There were reports that one of the main organizers of the "Unite the Right" event that led to the violence in Charlottesville once supported Obama and was involved in the left-wing "Occupy" movement. [11]

This isn't surprising. In his 1975 book, *Klandestine: The Untold Story of Delmar Dennis and His Role in the FBI's War Against the Ku Klux Klan*, William. H. McIlhaney II writes about KKK Grand Wizard Sam H. Bowers Jr. having been a member of the Communist Party USA before he brought the use of communist tactics to the white hate organization. Dennis was an FBI informant in the KKK.

Obama's Secretary of Homeland Security, Jeh Johnson, went on television to say that the removal of Confederate monuments and statues around the country had become a matter of "public safety and homeland security." It seemed like a threat or a warming.

Interestingly, Johnson is yet another Obama official with communism in his family or background. His grandfather, Charles S. Johnson, president of predominantly black Fisk University, was called upon to testify before the House Committee on Un-American Activities because of communist infiltration of Fisk and other black colleges. [12]

Ironically, as noted by conservative Catholic writer Vic Biorseth, the Democratic Party, which was, historically, the Party of the Confederacy, led the way in denouncing the pro-Confederate protesters and has become the chosen vehicle for the fundamental transformation of America.[13] He adds, regarding the violence in Charlottesville:

> Trump's immediate response to the incident was to condemn the violence on all sides. A

perfectly proper thing to do. And then he was attacked by "conservative" voices of even Trump supporters who don't know how fooled they themselves have been by Cultural Marxism.

He condemned all sides? How horrible! He should have condemned the white racist faction only.

I heard multiple "conservative" voices saying the President could have and should have tamped down the situation with a "carefully crafted statement," meaning politically corrected, condemning the Klan, the Nazis and the Alt-Right, whatever that means.

But President Trump is not "politically correct," thanks be to God. What he said was perfectly correct. It wasn't just the so-called Alt-Right group that came to Charlottesville from somewhere else spoiling for a fight.

Everyone who calls these people Right instead of Left has been mal-educated. Nazism is National Socialism, Marxist, and Leftist.

All these white racists are actually just as Marxist as the people who want to tear down all the Southern Civil War Monuments, and they don't even know it. They are all products of the same education system.

The only person who was open, honest and truthful, and most correct, in this whole incident was President Donald J. Trump. As usual.

Before Charlottesville, we had warned in our book *Comrade Obama Unmasked* about the violence to come.

We noted that the "Left Forum Conference 2017" was held June 2-4 in New York City, with the proclamation, "A powerful resistance is taking shape in the U.S. Mass spontaneous protests fill the streets and the opposition to the Trump regime heralds an era of civil unrest the likes of which America has not seen for decades." The Socialism 2017 conference was held in Chicago, Illinois, from July 6-9, with the admonition, "Build the Left" and "Fight the Right." One of the featured talks was, "100 Years of Revolutionary Struggle: From Russia to Today."

Such "revolutionary struggle" in the 1960s and 70s included terrorism directed by foreign powers, primarily in Moscow and Havana. This book is, in part, an effort to describe these forces and their influence on President Obama. Cuba, of course, is still officially communist, while Russia has dropped the communist label, in a move that has all the earmarks of a dialectical maneuver designed to confuse the world about what is actually happening under former KGB colonel Vladimir Putin.

Americans may have forgotten that many key terrorists who laid siege to America in the 1970s and 1980s in the name of liberating the U.S. from the capitalist system were never brought to justice. Some of them, such as Weather Underground terrorists Bill Ayers and Bernardine Dohrn, became professors and populated universities that we called *Marxist Madrassas.* Now "retired," Ayers has just written *Demand the Impossible!: A Radical Manifesto,* encouraging young people to be cannon fodder in the next phase of the revolution.

Tragically, as we described at our June 27, 2011, conference, "Traitors, Spies and Terrorists: America's Internal Security Crisis," congressional liberals abolished congressional committees investigating internal security and un-American activities. What's more, recent FBI directors such as James Comey and Robert S. Mueller have been proven incapable of effectively investigating terrorist networks. Mueller, the Russia-gate Special Counsel, blamed al Qaeda's post-9/11 anthrax attacks on innocent American scientists.

As we demonstrated in *Comrade Obama Unmasked,* the FBI still claims not to understand the motive behind Marxist James Hodgkinson's attempt to massacre a group of Republicans in Alexandria, Virginia, outside of Washington, D.C., in June. The FBI says he had an "anger" problem.

When the FBI was led by J. Edgar Hoover, extremist movements of the left and right were monitored, infiltrated, and even disrupted by the Bureau. The online "vault" maintained by the FBI features hundreds of pages of FBI efforts to undermine "white hate" groups, [14] including the Ku Klux Klan. "Today," the Bureau notes, "it's a shadow of its brazen, lawless self in the 1950s and 1960s -- thanks in large part to the dogged work of the FBI and its partners during that era…" [15] The now-defunct House Committee on Un-American Activities (HCUA) in 1965 conducted major hearings into the activities of Ku Klux Klan organizations in the U.S. At the same time, of course, the FBI and HUAC investigated communist activities.

The Workers World Party (WWP) was investigated by the now-defunct House Internal Security Committee for its support of the North Korean regime and Arab terrorist groups and today participates openly in confrontations like the one in Charlottesville, declaring that its veteran operative Sara Flounders was "a participant" in the "anti-racist mobilization." [16] As I discussed in the Center for Security Policy book, *Putin's Reset,* WWP operative Flounders was a speaker at the 2014 "Rhodes Forum," which is sponsored by Vladimir Putin's close associate and former KGB official Vladimir Yakunin. [17]

The WWP also showed up in Ferguson, Missouri, in 2014, when there was an unprovoked attack on a white policeman by a black thug named Michael Brown, who was high on drugs, and black protests and riots took place. Other outside agitators came from the Revolutionary Communist Party (RCP), whose chairman, Bob Avakian, is a communist who came out of Students for a Democratic Society.

There is a crying need for official investigations into these groups and their networks. Any such probe, however, should examine former President Obama and his communist associates.

In an interview with Radio New Zealand's Kathryn Ryan, Obama biographer David J. Garrow said that he started researching his monumental biography of Barack Obama's early years during the presidential campaign in 2008 because the media were not doing its job of vetting Obama. He said, "I was disappointed at how poor the journalism on Barack Obama's life story was. I was initially embarrassed that I knew so little about him, and he'd been a U.S. Senator for coming up on four years at that time." [18] We were disappointed as well. Unfortunately, his book is also a big disappointment.

His title, "Rising Star," is a phrase that was repeated ad nauseam by the liberal media.

In one respect, Garrow does offer some new and important information. Trent focused on the important new details in Garrow's book about Obama's relationship with Bill Ayers and Bernardine Dohrn. In 2008, she notes, Obama tried to deny his close personal and professional relationship with Ayers. Obama said, "This is a guy who lives in my neighborhood, who's a professor of English in Chicago who I know and who I have not received some official endorsement from. He's not somebody who I exchange ideas with on a regular basis. And the notion that somehow as a consequence of me knowing somebody who engaged in detestable acts 40 years ago, when I was 8 years old, somehow reflects on me and my values, doesn't make much sense."

In what she calls the most significant disclosure in *Rising Star*, Garrow fully demolishes these claims, describing "almost nightly dinners" for nearly a decade with the Obamas at the Ayers/Dohrn home or the house of Rashid and Mona Khalidi. By spring of 1996, Barack and Michelle were a regular presence at the two couples' "very informal" dinners (page 569 of *Rising Star*). Obama friend Rashid Khalidi, the pro-Palestinian Edward Said Professor of Arab Studies at Columbia, was once identified as a spokesman for the Palestine Liberation Organization (PLO), a group created by the Soviet KGB and whose long-time chairman, Yasser Arafat, was an agent of the Soviet intelligence service.

What is the significance of Obama's lie? It demonstrates his deep involvement in the communist network that spawned terrorism on U.S. soil and his desire to keep that information hidden from the American people. This is how a "mole" operates.

But rather than just being 1960s "radicals," Ayers and Dohrn were members of a Marxist-Leninist communist group. The Weather Underground, or Weathermen, wasn't just home-grown and domestic in nature, although it had evolved from the so-called Students for a Democratic Society (SDS), which laid siege to college campuses and tried to take over administration buildings. Their openly proclaimed goal was world communism. "We're revolutionary communists," Ayers himself said in 1969. The group received terrorist training in Communist Cuba and was advised by Soviet and Cuban intelligence agents.

Former FBI agent Max Noel, a member of the Weatherman Task Force in San Francisco, was among those who discovered the Weather Underground bomb factory in that city. It contained the fingerprints of Bill Ayers. FBI agents found dozens of copies of Marxist-Leninist books and pamphlets in the bomb factory, but did not locate any "anti-war" literature. In addition to C-4 explosives and dynamite, photos of what was confiscated show stabbing instruments used to stab people, not property.[19]

According to the FBI, which used to monitor communist groups, the Weather Underground had more contacts abroad than the Moscow-controlled Communist Party USA. Declassified intelligence information [20] reveals that the Weather Underground had connections not only to the CPUSA and foreign communist regimes, but even the Soviet KGB. The information shows that Ayers's and Dohrn's close terrorist associate, Kathy Boudin, attended Moscow University and was subsidized by the Soviet government. Her father was a CPUSA member and a registered Cuban agent.

During their time in the Weather Underground, before they became "respectable" and "mainstream" and associated with politicians like Barack Obama, Dohrn and Ayers signed a document, "Prairie Fire: The Politics of Revolutionary Anti-Imperialism," dedicated to Sirhan Sirhan, the Marxist assassin of Robert F. Kennedy. Dohrn, perhaps even more notorious than Ayers, once praised mass murderer Charles Manson as a "true revolutionary" and declared, "Dope is one of our weapons." Weather Underground member Mark Rudd, in his book, reminisces about his sexual promiscuity, involvement in bombings, and LSD trips. He became a prominent member of "Progressives for Obama."

As we noted back in 2008, before Obama was elected to his first term, an FBI report cited the "foreign influences" on the Weather Underground and said the organization was "carrying out the policies and purposes" of the communist Vietnamese and Cuban governments. The FBI said that the "Venceremos Brigade" trips to Cuba were organized by the Weather Underground "with the encouragement and instructions of the Cuban government." In short, there was Cuban direction of this communist terrorist group.

Many members of the Weather Underground, including Dohrn, traveled to Cuba, sometimes to meet with the Vietnamese communists, and others went directly to Hanoi, North Vietnam. One of their stated objectives was to prevent the U.S. from stopping a communist takeover of Vietnam. They succeeded, with the acquiescence of a liberal Congress, which cut off U.S. aid to the South Vietnamese government, and more than 58,000 American soldiers died in vain. The collapse of the South Vietnamese government paved the way for communist "re-education" camps housing hundreds of thousands of people, with many more thousands escaping as "boat people." The communist Khmer Rouge proceeded to take control of neighboring Cambodia and 1-2 million were slaughtered or forced to die there.

"Historically," according to the declassified U.S. Government intelligence information regarding the communist and foreign connections of the Weather Underground, "the United States has been the target of subversive efforts directed by the international communist movement to foment disorder and disruption in a revolutionary vein. These efforts were channeled into this country through the activities of communist-bloc diplomatic establishments and old-line communist groups and organizations working to advance international communist objectives. These old-line communist groups included the Communist Party U.S.A. (CPUSA), the Progressive Labor Party (PLP), and the Socialist Worker's Party (SWP)." [21]

The information declared, "The emergence of the New Left and black extremist movements in our society drastically altered the situation posed by old-line communist organizations. They evolved mostly out of social reform movements which were transformed into hard-core revolutionary movements dedicated to the total destruction of our democratic traditions and our society. They produced a new breed of revolutionaries whose main preoccupation with communism was that it produced men like Mao Tse-tung, Ho Chi Minh, and Che Guevara, whom they hoped to emulate in the overthrow of a system they deemed oppressive."

As president, reflecting his allegiance to this network, Obama's Justice Department released from prison Ayers associate Marilyn Buck, a member of the Weather Underground and the Black Liberation Army, which carried out a robbery of a Brinks truck in 1981 that killed two policemen and a security guard. Buck had been serving a prison term in California for her involvement in a long list of terrorist crimes. She was given early release from federal prison by Obama Attorney General Holder, who was deputy attorney general in the Clinton administration and involved in pardons for members of the Weather Underground at that time. Those released by President Clinton included Linda Evans and Susan Rosenberg, as well as members of the Cuban-supported terrorist group, the FALN. The Obama/Holder Justice Department falsely claimed that Buck had repented for her terrorist ways and called her release medically justified.

The Obama Justice Department also intervened to release terrorist lawyer Lynne Stewart from a federal prison. She had been sentenced to 10 years in prison for violating the law against supporting terrorism. She had provided illegal support to her client, the "Blind Sheik" Omar Abdel-Rahman, mastermind of the 1993 World Trade Center bombing. Stewart was given a "compassionate release" because it was said that she was suffering from a life-threatening disease.

**Freeing Communist Spies**

One of Ayers' associates released during the Clinton years, Weather Underground terrorist Linda Evans, spoke at a function hosted by the Cuban embassy in Washington, D.C., where she called on the assembled activists to urge Obama to release not only identified Cuban intelligence operatives in prison -- members of the so-called "Cuban Five" -- but also Puerto Rican terrorists like Oscar Lopez Rivera. This event was held on June 6, 2014, just a few blocks from the White House, in the basement of a black Baptist church.

Evans said, "We have some opportunities coming up for our federal prisoners, I believe, because of Obama and the fact that it's going to be his second and last term. And we need to create campaigns and participate in existing campaigns that can really take advantage of that. Some of our political prisoners are in federal custody."

All of this came to pass. Obama released Cuban spies imprisoned in the U.S. for various crimes, including participating in a murder conspiracy, in exchange for American Alan Gross, who had been held hostage by the Cuban regime for over five years. Gross was a foreign aid worker imprisoned by the Castro regime for trying to help ordinary Cubans communicate with the outside world. President Obama confirmed the role of Pope Francis in the sordid deal.

Later, Obama commuted the federal sentence of FALN terrorist leader and founder Oscar Lopez Rivera. The FALN claimed responsibility for over 140 bombings, including the infamous January 24, 1975, lunchtime attack on Fraunces Tavern in New York City which killed four innocent people.

To those who would balk at this characterization of our 44th president as a covert communist, we urge a close reading of the piece, "Mandela and Communism," from the Communist *People's World* newspaper. Although the article was about the South African president Nelson Mandela, exposed as a member of the South African Communist Party after his death, the author, Rick Nagin, compares Mandela to Barack Obama. Published on December 13, 2013, after Obama's election to a second term, Nagin said communist revolutions go through various stages and that, in the U.S., the "Democratic parts of the ruling class" were "still very much needed" for communism to succeed here. Nagin, a veteran Communist Party official, urged support for President Obama and "the Obama coalition," in order to prevent division in the ranks of the progressives. He said to "win at this stage we need to emulate the steadfastness and political maturity shown by Mandela and the South African Communist Party."

**Infiltration of the Democratic Party**

The reference to "Democratic parts of the ruling class" means the Democratic Party. President Reagan told journalist Arnaud de Borchgrave in a 1987 interview that "I've been a student of the communist movement for a long time, having been a victim of it some years ago in Hollywood," and that he regarded some two dozen Marxists in Congress as "a problem we have to face." The problem is far worse today. Analyst Trevor Loudon now counts the number of Marxists in Congress at more than 60, working through the

Congressional Progressive Caucus and the Democratic Party.

Indeed, Obama is the culmination of a decades-long attempt to infiltrate the Democratic Party. As Trevor says in the foreword to *Comrade Obama Unmasked*, "How a covert communist was able to gain the presidency of the United States of America, hiding his true nature from more than 300 million Americans, will occupy scholars for years." This is one reason why we are closely examining Garrow's book. Any new information about Obama has to be reviewed and understood.

In his report, "From Henry Wallace to William Ayers -- the Communist and Progressive Movements," the late Herbert Romerstein points out that while Henry Wallace wasn't a communist, his third party movement in 1948, the Progressive Party, was under Communist Party control. "The Communists even reassigned some of their members from Soviet espionage to run the Progressive Party," he noted. The CPUSA was funded by Moscow and was so obedient to the Soviet line that it backed the Hitler–Stalin pact.

Wallace was not an insignificant figure, having been vice president in Franklin Roosevelt's third term.

Romerstein notes that Earl Browder, who headed the Communist Party in the 1930s until 1945, had boasted in 1960 about the success of the communists under his leadership. Browder had said:

Entering the 1930's as a small ultra-left sect of some 7,000 members, remnant of the fratricidal factional struggle of the 1920's that had wiped out the old "left wing" of American socialism, the CP rose to become a national political influence far beyond its numbers (at its height it never exceeded 100,000 members), on a scale never before reached by a socialist movement claiming the Marxist tradition. It became a practical power in organized labor, its influence became strong in some state organizations of the Democratic Party (even dominant in a few for some years), and even some Republicans solicited its support. It guided the anti-Hitler movement of the American League for Peace and Democracy that united a cross-section of some five million organized Americans (a list of its sponsors and speakers would include almost a majority of Roosevelt's Cabinet, the most prominent intellectuals, judges of all grades up to State Supreme Courts, church leaders, labor leaders, etc.). Right-wing intellectuals complained that it exercised an effective veto in almost all publishing houses against their books, and it is at least certain that those right-wingers had extreme difficulty getting published.

In this context, a far more questionable treatment of the socialist or "progressive" movement can be found in a lengthy report issued by the Center for American Progress (CAP) entitled "The Progressive Intellectual Tradition in America." Curiously, it ignores Henry

Wallace and his communist-dominated Progressive Party.

I asked John Halpin, who wrote much of the CAP report and also co-authored *The Power of Progress* with John Podesta, then CAP's president, about this omission. He replied:

> Henry Wallace received fewer votes than Dixiecrat Strom Thurmond in 1948 and carried no states. Nearly all progressive and liberal support went to Harry Truman. Wallace was a decent man and his work on agriculture and his stands on ending segregation and fighting for racial equality were admirable. However, because of his foreign policy stands and his naive approach to Communist influence in the party, most of the major progressive and liberal voices of the time—including Eleanor Roosevelt, John Kenneth Galbraith, Arthur Schlesinger, Jr., and Reinhold Niebuhr -- gathered within Americans for Democratic Action, an explicitly anti-Communist, pro-civil rights organization. Long term, Wallace's 1948 campaign had no real impact on progressives.

But while the Dixiecrats faded from the scene, the "progressives" did not. This is a critical point.

Noted historian and author David Pietrusza confirms this, telling me:

Following their humiliating 1948 defeat, Wallace's Progressives refused to surrender. They instead embarked upon a "Long March" that led to their ideological heirs' capture of the modern Democratic Party. A key milestone in their re-birth was 1968. That year, Democrats turned against Truman-JFK-LBJ Cold War policies. That same year, former Progressive Party national convention delegate Senator George McGovern emerged as the heir to the martyred Robert Kennedy. Four years later, McGovern captured the Democratic nomination and re-wrote party national convention rules to cement the transformation of his party's leftward drift. The Obama victory of 2008, and the personnel and policies of his administration, largely translate into a victory for Henry Wallace's ideological heirs, not for Truman's. The Truman-style Democrat is largely extinct.

Halpin's reference to Wallace's "naive approach to Communist influence in the party" suggests recognition that communism was and is a danger and that Wallace was not sufficiently alert to this problem. But is this the case with the modern-day progressive movement? CAP's employment of "former" communist Van Jones and his rehiring, after details about his communist background had emerged -- suggests it is not.

The non-communists like Wallace who tolerated communists became known as "fellow travelers" or dupes. The Communists used such people to influence non-communist Americans in the trade union movement and the Democratic Party.

Romerstein notes, "Two secret Communist Party members became Democratic members of the United States Congress. They were John Bernard from Minnesota and Hugh DeLacy from Washington State. A 'friend of the Party' was Vito Marcantonio, who was elected to Congress first as a Republican, then as a Democrat, and finally as a candidate of the Communist Party controlled American Labor Party in New York."

In *Comrade Obama Unmasked,* we asked a former Intelligence Community insider about the significance of Obama. Here is an excerpt:

> Kincaid: …Is what we're looking at here a successful effort by Moscow to place one of their agents in the White House?
>
> Insider: Sure. They wanted to do that with Henry Wallace.
>
> Kincaid: So Obama is really a successful update of Henry Wallace. But Wallace was a candidate of the Progressive Party. Obama ran as a Democrat. Let's bring it up to date. We had eight years of Obama. He damaged the United States. But his designated successor loses on November 8, 2016. Donald Trump is taking over a government that has been thoroughly infiltrated. What does he do to dig us out of this mess?

Insider: He will have to start a long-term project. The Republican Party has never recognized this Soviet influence in the political process. They have not struggled against it. They just don't seem to recognize Communist Party operations. I don't think the party itself is capable of understanding the communist challenge in ideological and operational terms. Until they're enlightened, they can't make progress.

A semi-official history of the Progressive Party, in the form of the book, *Gideon's Army,* was written by Curtis MacDougall, a professor of journalism at Northwestern University who also wrote *Interpretative Reporting,* a standard text in journalism schools for more than 50 years. MacDougall, who wrote critically (even in his journalism textbook) about efforts to expose communist influence in the U.S. Government, was himself a Progressive Party activist and candidate.

**Educating Progressive Journalists**

Not surprisingly, MacDougall's influence was felt not only on generations of journalists, but on his own son, A. Kent MacDougall, who was acknowledged in the 1972 edition of *Interpretative Reporting* as then being with the New York office of the *Wall Street Journal* and lending "valuable assistance" in its preparation. Kent came out openly as a Marxist after working at the *Journal,* where he said he inserted positive stories about Marxist economists and "the left-wing journalist

I.F. Stone." Stone, it turned out, was a Soviet agent of influence.

MacDougall's 319-page FBI file, released to this journalist, revealed that he had a close association with the *Chicago Star,* a newspaper controlled by the Communist Party, and many different CPUSA front organizations. But the *Star* connection deserves special comment. The executive editor of the *Chicago Star* was none other than Frank Marshall Davis, a Communist Party member who would later become President Barack Obama's childhood mentor in Hawaii and was active in the Hawaii Democratic Party.

In 1948, notes historian David Pietrusza, Davis's Chicago-based paper, *the Chicago Star,* wholeheartedly backed Henry Wallace. That summer, he adds, the Progressive Party "apparatus" converted the paper into the *Illinois Standard,* thus enabling Davis to relocate to Hawaii on the advice of fellow Progressive Party activist Paul Robeson. Robeson, it turned out, was a secret member of the Communist Party.

It is significant that MacDougall's history of the Progressive Party, *Gideon's Army,* was published by Italian-born American Communist Carl Marzani, who served a prison term for perjury in falsely denying, while employed by the State Department, that he was a Communist Party member. His publishing house, Marzani and Munsell, was subsidized by the Soviet KGB.

Lt. Gen. Ion Mihai Pacepa, the highest-ranking official ever to have defected from the former Soviet bloc, said in an article for PJMedia that any doubt that the Democratic and the Communist parties had secretly joined forces was erased in 2009, "when Van Jones, part of a left fringe of declared communists, became the White House's green jobs czar." Pacepa, who served as a top aide in the Romanian communist regime, told me, "The Democratic Party has become dangerously infected with the Marxism virus. I recognize the symptoms because I once lived through them, and I believe it is my obligation as an American citizen to help the conservative movement to prevent any further spread of Marxism in my adopted country."

He added that he was personally convinced that Obama is a Marxist.

**The Mandela Strategy**

Communist operative Rick Nagin's article comparing Mandela and Obama was an endorsement of deception in order to further socialist goals. Has Obama concealed his communist ties in the same way Mandela covered-up his own Communist Party membership? This is one reason why we need a full-blown official investigation of the former president.

Interestingly, Obama tweeted quotes from Nelson Mandela after the violent clashes in Charlottesville, Virginia, in August that left three people dead, including a pedestrian killed when a car plowed into a group of "anti-fascist" protesters. "No one is born hating another person because of the color of his skin or his background or his religion ... People must learn to hate, and if they can learn to hate, they can be taught to love... ...For love comes more naturally to the human heart than its opposite," Obama said in a series of three tweets. Obama's response was dubbed the "Most Liked Tweet of all Time."

Quoting Mandela was significant and misleading. Obama was himself taught to hate. His communist mentor, Frank Marshall Davis, was a black racist who saw sinister white plots in the foreign policies of the United States and other Western nations. Obama's own book, *Dreams from My Father,* talks about asking "Frank" for advice when his white grandmother had been accosted by a black panhandler. Davis told Obama that his grandmother was right to be scared and that "She understands that black people have reason to hate."

Obama has to know that the communists who run South Africa today and put Mandela in power are pursuing a Soviet-style strategy of revolutionary change. Despite his at times flowery language and apparent devotion to a "rainbow nation," Mandela lied about his South African Communist Party (SACP) membership for decades and millions of people were fooled by him. He lied in order to rope in what are called "dupes" to the communist cause. It is a well-established strategy by communists, using front groups. In the case of South Africa, the SACP used the African National Congress (ANC), headed by Mandela. It was a perfect relationship, designed to fool foreign audiences, because Mandela was involved with both organizations.

As Alex Newman notes in our book, *Comrade Obama Unmasked*, Jacob Zuma, the current president of South Africa and a well-documented member of the Communist Party, today sings "genocidal songs" directed against the white minority. Newman reports:

> Consider that President Zuma celebrated the ANC's centenary anniversary in 2012 by going on national TV and singing a genocidal song advocating the slaughter of the white Boers in front of his military. "Power for us," Zuma sang, as a fake sign-language interpreter, later implicated in atrocities, meaninglessly gesticulated next to him. "We are going to shoot them with the machine gun, they are going to run. You are a Boer, shoot the Boer."

**The Continuing Cover-Up**

In order to highlight media misdeeds and promote a free and open press, we have stressed that the reclusive Matt Drudge, supposedly a conservative, suppressed information we developed on Obama's communist connections in Hawaii and Chicago. If his Drudge Report had published this information, in the form of advertising we tried to take out on his site, the results of the November 2008 election could have been different. It was Drudge who had played a role in the impeachment of Bill Clinton by publicizing *Newsweek's* suppressed story of the stained blue dress which proved that, despite his denials, Clinton had engaged in an extramarital affair with a White House intern.

In regard to Obama's communist connections, Drudge could have turned the tide politically through accepting our advertising about the communists backing Obama. Instead, Drudge helped bring Obama to power by suppressing this critical information.

This was one reason why, in 2013, we published *The Crisis in American Journalism and the Conservative Response,* and held a conference on this matter at the National Press Club in Washington, D.C. Tina Trent was a speaker and co-author. She spoke on the subject of "Matt Drudge: the King of Conservative Media?," looking at his strange background and tendency to create confusion among conservative media listeners, readers, and viewers.

To cite one notorious example of the liberal media bias on this topic, Obama biographer and *Washington Post* reporter David Maraniss wrote a 10,000-word piece for the *Post* in 2008, when the information could have made a difference in the campaign, ignoring the fact that communist Frank Marshall Davis was Obama's mentor in Hawaii and the mysterious "Frank" from Obama's book, *Dreams from My Father.*

Maraniss had all the essential details and could have broken the story wide open. We later learned why the potential blockbuster story about Obama's Communist mentor was deliberately ignored by Maraniss. He had personal and political conflicts that prevented him from telling the truth about Obama to the American people. Simply put, his parents were Communists, just like Davis.

The good news is that conservative alternative networks are becoming more widely available through the emergence of Internet streaming devices such as Roku. The success of our ASI Roku TV channel demonstrates the hunger that exists for alternative news and information. With Roku, you can bypass cable and satellite TV, saving money. Roku uses an Internet connection to broadcast TV channels.

Our YouTube channel, now with almost 1.8 million views, features important speeches from our conferences, including those of Larry Grathwohl, former FBI informant in the Weather Underground.

In prescient remarks to our videotaped October 27, 2011, America's Survival conference, Larry urged congressional scrutiny of Obama Administration links to the "Occupy Wall Street" movement and related mobs, which include assorted Marxists, communists, socialists and anarchists. "Let this be a teaching moment as to how the violence of the 1960s and 70s that I witnessed first-hand can return with a vengeance," he said. "Let us hope that we act and stop this madness before it is too late."

In an interview on America's Survival TV, Larry's daughter, Lindsay Grathwohl, said she fears the return of a terrorist movement like the Weather Underground.

Lindsay has had to wear helmets and eye protectors at free speech rallies which have come under assault from bricks, rocks, and bottles thrown by far-left Antifa demonstrators trained in buildings owned by local affiliates of the Service Employees International Union (SEIU).

Predicting a theme we see Antifa using to generate confrontations, Larry had spoken at one of our conferences on the significance of a 2009 book by Obama associates Bill Ayers and Bernardine Dohrn entitled, *Race Course Against White Supremacy.* Grathwohl said Ayers and Dohrn regarded Obama, whose political career they sponsored, as a tool -- a puppet -- to use against and provoke white America.

As we saw in Charlottesville, the communists use the threat of white supremacy to justify their own violent reaction to it. This seems like a logical revolutionary follow-up to the creation of Black Lives Matter, which had openly declared that cop-killer Assata Shakur was very "important" to their cause and had nevertheless been invited into the Obama White House.

Grathwohl understood the role that minorities were to play in the revolution when he was assigned to Detroit, Michigan, in order to bomb a police station. Shortly after his arrival there in late January of 1970, he was assigned to a cell with four other people, and during a meeting with Bill Ayers they were told "that our objective would be to place bombs at the Detroit Police Officers Association (DPOA Building) and at the 13th precinct." The DPOA building, Grathwohl discovered, was a converted single-family brownstone that had been built prior to World War II. Next to the DPOA building was a Red Barn restaurant, located in a predominantly black neighborhood, meaning that most of the customers were black.

He said, "After a week of information gathering we had another meeting with Bill Ayers and at this time I suggested to Bill that if we placed the bomb in the walkway between these two buildings, the DPOA building would suffer little if any damage while the Red Barn restaurant would most likely be destroyed. I also concluded that customers in that restaurant would die."

Grathwohl said Ayers told him, "Sometimes innocent people have to die in a revolution." Grathwohl commented, "I was shocked. I couldn't believe that a person who had so eloquently spoken of the black liberation movement could be so callous when it was obvious that the resulting explosion would kill many of the people he claimed to be so concerned about."

Grathwohl was told by Bill Ayers in February of 1970 that Bernardine Dohrn was the main perpetrator of the bombing of the Park Police Station which resulted in the death of Sgt. Brian V. McDonnell. This bombing had significant similarities to the planned bombing of the Detroit police officers Association building and 13th precinct in that city in February 1970. "Having infiltrated the Weather Underground, I was involved in the planning of these bombings," Grathwohl said. "Bill Ayers gave specific instructions on how the bomb was to be built and when and where it was to be placed. This included the use of fence nails and staples to act as shrapnel, that the bomb was to be place during a shift change, and that it would be placed on a window ledge. All of these so-called coincidences are the same as what occurred at the Park Station in February of 1970. These [other] bombs failed to detonate; otherwise several deaths would have occurred as was clearly emphasized by Bill Ayers during the planning sessions for these actions."

The bomb that killed three of their own members when it accidentally exploded in a New York townhouse was an anti-personnel device intended for an Army dance at Fort Dix, New Jersey. Mark Rudd, another member of the Weather Underground, revealed that he was in favor of planting the bomb, saying that he wanted "this country to have a taste of what it had been dishing out daily in Southeast Asia..." What the U.S. had been trying to do was prevent a communist takeover of South Vietnam.

The terrorists managed to avoid responsibility for most of their crimes because the Jimmy Carter Justice Department indicted and charged FBI officials with violating the civil rights of the terrorists and their associates. Recognizing the political prosecution of the FBI officials as a terrible miscarriage of justice, President Reagan would later pardon them.

A law enforcement entity known as the Phoenix Task Force was dismantled in 2011, before it could solve the cold case bombing murder of San Francisco Police

Sergeant McDonnell. It was made up of law enforcement personal, including representatives from the FBI, the California Department of Justice and the San Francisco Police Department. The Justice Department can and should reopen the case.

**Obama's Comrades**

On one level, Obama comes across in the Garrow book as a typical politician. For example, Garrow discusses Obama's address to the Chicago Council on Foreign Relations (page 930), where he singled out Iran as a "dangerous cheater in the nuclear game." This is set forth in a matter of fact way, when history shows that Obama's nuclear deal with Iran will, at best, only temporarily curtail the regime's nuclear weapons program.

These policies, combined with the evidence of contacts between the Obama White House and the pro-terrorist Muslim Brotherhood, lead to the inescapable conclusion that his anti-American foreign policy was designed to enable America's enemies in the communist and Muslim worlds to either obtain nuclear weapons or stay on the road to acquiring them.

Garrow mentions that Rep. Danny Davis (D-Ill.) backed Obama, without citing the evidence of Davis's service to the Communist Party. In 2012, America's Survival, Inc. honored Jeremy Segal, a disciple of the late Andrew Breitbart, who produced a video of Davis being honored by the *People's World* at the Communist Party headquarters in Chicago for a lifetime of "inspiring leadership." At the time, Davis served on the Homeland Security Committee where his subcommittee assignments were the Subcommittee on Transportation and the Subcommittee on Oversight. He is also a member of the Congressional Progressive Caucus.

When Segal started questioning the congressman outside the CPUSA headquarters, communists as well as a Davis handler wearing an Obama jacket tried to intervene to protect Davis from further questioning, with one person calling Segal "disgusting."

The so-called "rest of the story" about Davis, one of many examples we could cite, fills out much of the story about the "rising star" described in Garrow's book.

What we already know is that Obama was only the proverbial tip of the iceberg. In the matter of the network of current and former officials he picked for his administration, we also find serious gaps in the Garrow work. For example, Garrow has only two references to Leon Panetta, who served as Obama's Secretary of Defense and CIA director, both of them quoting critical comments from Panetta about Obama.

Yet, Panetta was a key Obama hire who was plugged into the same networks which spawned Obama. Trevor Loudon and I worked on the Panetta case extensively.

Panetta had inserted a tribute in the April 11, 1984, Congressional Record to one of his constituents, Lucy Haessler, calling her a "woman of peace" for her work in the pro-Soviet Women's International League for Peace and Freedom (WILPF). This is when Panetta was a California Congressman representing Santa Cruz. Panetta also declared that Haessler participated in "peace conferences" sponsored by another group, the Women's International Democratic Federation, "in France, the Soviet Union, Poland, and East Germany." One has to wonder about the "peace conferences" being held in such places as the Soviet Union. But Panetta put the tribute in the record without displaying any indication of its Soviet sponsorship or casting doubt on the organization's commitment to "peace."

Panetta's praise for Haessler got the attention at the time of *Human Events,* the national conservative weekly, which noted that WILPF "appears to take the Soviet line on virtually every issue that comes up, ranging from the Soviet invasion of Afghanistan and yellow rain [communist chemical warfare] to the issue of new U.S. missiles in Europe." The Women's International Democratic Federation was an outright Soviet front organization.

Panetta told *Human Events* that he was unaware of the extremist nature of the WILPF and other groups, but indicated it wouldn't have mattered that much to him anyway. He said, "Let me tell you something. I don't know if you know about Santa Cruz, but Santa Cruz is a center for people who've been real activists in all kinds of organizations. If I started doing those kinds of checks on people who help out…I'd never stop. It's just that kind of place."

Panetta's tribute to identified Communist Party member Hugh DeLacy, inserted into the Congressional Record in 1983, suggests that Panetta did have keen knowledge of these "real activists," by virtue of his praise for DeLacy's stand against "McCarthyism." Hence, it appears that Panetta did indeed "check" on these people, completely understood they had been accused of membership in the Communist Party or having communist sympathies, and found them totally acceptable and praiseworthy.

The series of "Dear Hugh" and "Dear Leon" letters discovered by Trevor Loudon in the Hugh DeLacy papers at the University of Washington proves that Panetta had a working and cordial relationship with him. In fact, Panetta provided DeLacy, a key contact of a communist spy ring, with sensitive documents. And judging from the tone of some of the letters, DeLacy appeared to be telling Panetta what to say and do as a sitting member of Congress. Even after Panetta attended a private "celebration" for DeLacy and his wife Dorothy, another communist, DeLacy reminded Panetta that he should return to scrutinizing the "military boondoggle."

The tribute to Haessler proved that the DeLacy controversy is not a fluke but part of a disturbing pattern. In 1979, Panetta had spoken in Santa Cruz when the local chapter of WILPF was the site and host of the organization's national congress.

"For 20 years, she [Lucy Haessler] and her late husband Carl conducted a public education campaign to impress upon all Americans the folly of U.S. military involvement in that region of the world," Panetta said, referring to Indochina.

Panetta was a consistent opponent of U.S. military efforts to resist communism in such critical regions of the world as Indochina and Central America. He was a vociferous critic of President Reagan's use of the CIA to frustrate Soviet and Cuban designs on Nicaragua, where DeLacy and Panetta had both visited. DeLacy honored the Communist Sandinistas who had taken over the country while Panetta in 1983 sponsored a bill to terminate covert action against the Sandinistas.

After visiting Nicaragua, Panetta declared (Congressional Record, October 3, 1984) that he and his fellow members of Congress saw "real accomplishments" under the communists and that "The goal of the U.S. Government should be to normalize U.S.-Nicaraguan relations..." Panetta denounced what he called the "counter-revolutionary groups," the Marxist term for those Reagan had praised and supported as "freedom fighters."

After Reagan liberated Grenada from a band of communist thugs and rescued American students on the island, Panetta said in the Congressional Record (November 2, 1983) that support for the action from the American people should not be seen as a "blank check" and that it should remain "limited." Panetta said that he was very concerned that the Reagan Administration had dispatched a U.S. naval task force to the vicinity of Cuba as a show of force. Hence, Panetta was clearly concerned that the U.S.-backed forces of liberation would undermine and threaten the Castro dictatorship.

Tragically, President Trump has been left with a United States in such a weakened state that he had to seek passage of United Nations Resolution 2371, adopted by the Security Council on August 5, 2017, as a step forward against the Communist North Korean nuclear program. It seemed like another futile attempt to strengthen sanctions on North Korea. China and Russia voted for the resolution but are sponsors of and have "friendship" treaties with the communist regime.

As we have long argued, in our books *Global Bondage* and *Global Taxes for World Government*, the United Nations is a communist front and cannot effectively stop the communist advance. A real "America First" foreign policy has to entail withdrawing from the world body.

**The U.N. is a Communist Front Organization**

I wrote about a State Department document on the founding of the world organization, "The United States and the Founding of the United Nations, August 1941 – October 1945," which ignored the role of communist spy Alger Hiss in its founding. I filed a Freedom of Information Act (FOIA) request to find out why.

The material consists of 215 pages of internal State Department documents, including several drafts of the report, "The United States and the Founding of the United Nations, August 1941 – October 1945," which examines minor controversies over mostly trivial matters. The material constitutes an indictment of the State Department's failure to acknowledge, let alone explain, how a communist assumed a major position of authority and power in the State Department and then used that influence to create a world organization that has been exploited for anti-American purposes ever since.

The Organization of Islamic Cooperation (OIC) is one of the largest blocs of nations at the U.N. It includes 56 Islamic states promoting Muslim solidarity in economic, social, and political affairs. Russia is an OIC observer state. The OIC has called for critics of Islam to be silenced, on the grounds that such criticism constitutes "Islamophobia." President Obama told the U.N. that "The future must not belong to those who slander the prophet of Islam."

To complicate matters for Trump, Republican Senator John McCain, who was Barack Obama's opponent in the 2008 presidential campaign, has emerged as one of Trump's most vociferous critics. A *Washington Times* column by Allan H. Ryskind demonstrates that McCain started the Russia-gate investigation of Trump by providing the FBI with the largely discredited so-called Trump dossier. [22] Rowan Scarborough of the *Washington Times* wrote that the "Russian-fed" Trump dossier was written by former British intelligence agent Christopher Steele and "used Moscow disinformation to influence the presidential election against Donald Trump and attack his administration." [23]

At Accuracy in Media, I supervised the production of several reports on this matter, which we labeled "The Final Truth About the 'Trump Dossier.'"[24]

Our judgment is that Russia-gate is, in fact, a diversion from the Russian penetration of the national Democratic Party and Russian control over, even blackmail of, Obama.

The bizarre turn-about, a brilliant Marxist dialectical maneuver, was seen in the fact that Rep. Jamie Raskin, a Maryland Democrat and a vice chair of the Congressional Progressive Caucus, emerged as a major critic of Russian influence in the Trump Administration. His father was Marcus Raskin, a former Kennedy administration official who was a founder of the Marxist Institute for Policy Studies (IPS). In the 1980s, in order to undermine Reagan's defense buildup, Marcus Raskin and the IPS planned several conferences with Soviet officials believed to be under the influence or control of the Soviet intelligence services. At the time, 12 members of the U.S. Senate and 70 members of the House wrote to Secretary of State George Shultz, warning that the Soviet Union would use the events for intelligence purposes.

IPS subservience to the agenda of the Soviet Union and its client state was a major topic of concern to those backing Reagan's anti-Soviet policies.

Journalist and author Brian Crozier wrote in *National Review* that the IPS was "the perfect intellectual front for Soviet activities which would be resisted if they were to originate openly from the KGB." S. Steven Powell's book on the IPS, *Covert Cadre,* includes photographs of identified Soviet agents who attended IPS functions or associated with IPS personalities. He names two as KGB officers.

The IPS even hosted convicted Soviet spy Alger Hiss. It regarded him as innocent and launched a series of "Alger Hiss lectures" in 2002, after receiving a bequest from the estate of Alger and Isabel Johnson Hiss.

Ironically, Rep. Raskin used his D.C. speech to denounce the Russians for using "active measures" or influence operations against the United States, the same kind that his own father's organization facilitated.

It is not too late for CIA and FBI investigations into the former president. But the Intelligence Community has to be purged of enemy agents, spies, and moles.

Trump adviser and former campaign aide Sam Clovis had reportedly said the following about Barack Obama on radio shows or blogs:

> …beginning with his teen years, we find a person who indulged in self-destructive behavior. Further, he was directly influenced by a devout communist and pedophile in the personage of Frank Marshall Davis. How profound that influence might have been is certainly open for speculation, but it is clear that the Obama who went on to Occidental (how he got in is a mystery, as are his admittances to

Columbia and Harvard) was a young man who was well on his way to crafting the illusion that was quite different from his real life.

These remarks by Clovis were "discovered" by CNN, which considered them damaging to Clovis when he was nominated to a post in the Department of Agriculture. [25] But they show that the information we have released about Obama is being circulated in various circles, despite the efforts of liberal and conservative media to suppress it.

Still, millions of Americans are not aware of Obama's Marxist roots. That is why books this like are so necessary.

**Don't Ask, Don't Tell**

The Communist Party USA openly backed Obama for president in 2008 and 2012.

In his book, *Rising Star,* David Garrow mentions the influence of communist Frank Marshall Davis, who mentored Obama as a young man in Hawaii for eight years. But Garrow seems unfamiliar with our extensive body of work on the subject. He cites only one of my reports on Davis in his notes but never called me while preparing his book. Here are some of the basic facts about Davis:

- Davis was the subject of a 600-page FBI file.
- Davis was under FBI surveillance for 19 years for his Communist Party activities.

- Davis was on the FBI's security index, meaning he could be arrested in the event of a national emergency.
- The FBI found him taking photographs of the Hawaii coastline, apparently for espionage purposes.
- Davis wrote a pornographic novel, *Sex Rebel*, that was autobiographical and disclosed that he had sex with children.
- Davis was a heavy drinker and marijuana user.

Garrow calls Davis a dues-paying member of the Communist Party USA and a "sexual adventurer," an odd way to identity a sex pervert with a pornography obsession who wrote about having sex with children. He notes Davis's friendship with actor and singer Paul Robeson, the latter having "pro-communist views," without going the extra step and mentioning his membership in the CPUSA.

An additional detail about Obama's communist and Soviet connections that Garrow mentions in passing is his involvement as a young man in the international communist network known as CISPES, the Committee in Solidarity with the People of El Salvador. Garrow describes it as an organization opposing U.S. aid to El Salvador's military government. In fact, CISPES was committed to the victory of the communist FMLN in El Salvador and was founded in 1980 by leaders of the Communist Party USA, who met with Farid Handal, brother of the Salvadoran Communist chairman Shafik Handal. I wrote a lengthy report on the formation of CISPES for the April 25, 1981, *Human Events*.

Whether the issue was El Salvador or South Africa (as Alex Newman writes about in a chapter of our book *Comrade Obama Unmasked*), Obama could always be counted on to take the communist side, from his days as a student into his presidency.

This is why, as former FBI agent Max Noel told me, Obama could never pass the CARL test for federal employment by analyzing Character, Associates, Reputation, and Loyalty to the United States.

In this context, it is also significant to note that America's first openly Marxist big city mayor, Bill "Red Bill" de Blasio of New York City, started out as a supporter of the Communist Sandinistas in Nicaragua in the 1980s by raising money for the Nicaragua Solidarity Network. He did most of his work on behalf of the Sandinistas through the Quixote Center in Maryland, a group I came across while writing about the wars in Central America for *Human Events* in the 1980s. A spin-off, the Christic Institute, filed a frivolous lawsuit against supporters of the Nicaragua freedom fighters. You can still see my 1987 debate with Daniel Sheehan of the Christic Institute on C-SPAN.

When I noted the Communist links of the Christic Institute during the debate, Sheehan's predictable response was "Joe McCarthy." His frivolous lawsuit was thrown out of court in a case described as legal terrorism against anti-communists. The Quixote Center was founded by Catholic leaders, as even the *New York Times* pointed out, but these "leaders" were on the far left and dedicated to the belief that communism and

Christianity could mix. It is also known as liberation theology.

The *Times* reported, "In 1991, at one of his final meetings with the Nicaragua Solidarity Network, he [de Blasio] argued that the liberal values the group had defended were 'far from dead' around the world, with blossoming movements in places like Mexico, the Philippines, El Salvador and Brazil, according to minutes of the meeting. He spoke of a need to understand and build alliances with Islam, predicting it would soon be a dominant force in politics."

This alliance with Islam is precisely what has emerged, as we document in our book, *Red Jihad: Moscow's Final Solution for America and Israel.* It is significant that Carlos the Jackal, the terrorist trained by the KGB, converted to Islam and became devoted to Osama bin Laden.

Promoting a Marxist alliance with Islam, in view of 9/11 and the anti-American terrorism around the world, is something that takes on ominous and frightening implications. It is now being reported that some factions of the Taliban in Afghanistan have been receiving arms from Russia.

As former KGB officer Konstantin Preobrazhensky said in his ASI report, "Communists and Muslims: The Hidden Hand of the KGB," much of what passes for radical Islamic terrorism is made in Moscow.

When he first ran for mayor, in 2013, he had the endorsement of Barack Obama, who said, "Progressive change is the centerpiece of Bill de Blasio's vision for New York City, and it's why he will be a great mayor of America's largest city."

**De Blasio's Progressive Vision**

When de Blasio and Obama were involved with "solidarity committees" in El Salvador and Nicaragua, the communists were waging a violent, terrorist war for Central America. Author James L. Tyson documented how the American Catholic Church, working through Father J. Bryan Hehir and others, were on the communist side. Hehir in 1983 delivered a series of lectures at the far-left Institute for Policy Studies entitled, "Matthew, *Marx,* Luke, and John," illustrating the continuing left-wing drift of the Catholic Church.

At that time, the Institute for Policy Studies began promoting the "sanctuary movement," designed to facilitate the entry into the U.S. of illegal aliens who were supposedly being repressed by pro-American governments. IPS gave the sanctuary movement a "human rights" award in 1984. The U.S. Catholic Bishops supported the "sanctuary movement" and, in a statement in 1985, denounced the criminal indictments of those caught smuggling illegal aliens. Through the Catholic Campaign for Human Development, an arm of the Bishops, the church funded Casa de Maryland, an illegal alien support group.

Garrow also mentions Obama's relationship with pro-Soviet Illinois politician Alice Palmer. We had known about this, having published Trevor Loudon's 2012 report, "The Pro-Soviet Agent of Influence Who Gave Barack Obama His First Job in Politics." [26] Garrow refers to her "pro-Soviet sympathies," travels to the Soviet Union, and membership in the U.S. Peace Council, without noting that the latter was CPUSA-controlled and the American affiliate of the Soviet front World Peace Council. We discovered a document in the archives of the U.S. Peace Council showing that Palmer specialized in media manipulation for the communist front.

The conclusions of our report were that:

> Alice Palmer was a pro-communist activist working inside the Illinois Democratic Party. She worked closely with the future U.S. president for several years, in the same socialist and communist networks that dominated the left side of Chicago politics.
>
> Alice Palmer was also a high level, pro-Soviet operative, actively involved with known Soviet and communist front organizations at the height of the Cold War.
>
> She was a major proponent of Soviet "peace" initiatives primarily aimed at destroying NATO and disarming the United States.

> Now Alice Palmer's former protégé is the most powerful politician in the world.
>
> Interestingly, where Alice Palmer once worked tirelessly in the interests of the Soviet Union, Barack Obama seems to be working almost as enthusiastically to give the Russians what they want.
>
> Alice Palmer pushed Soviet "peace" proposals at the height of the Cold War. Now, in a different climate, Barack Obama has the power to carry out those policies and seems to be doing so.

Garrow ignores the real significance of people like Palmer and Rep. Davis in the start of Obama's political career. Obama's political career was nurtured by a communist network, first in Hawaii and then in Chicago. Garrow fails to explain the real significance of Obama's connections to the international Soviet-sponsored communist network and the fronts and terrorists involved in them.

Similarly, Garrow has two pages on Obama's close relationship with his CIA director John Brennan, without noting Brennan's service to the communist and Islamist cases. Brennan disclosed that he voted for the Communist Party ticket when he was in college. He was hired by the CIA anyway and quickly rose through the ranks, even though the CPUSA was funded by Moscow and known to provide cover for Soviet espionage activities. Brennan reportedly converted to Islam when he was stationed in Saudi Arabia.

Overall, as we demonstrate in *Comrade Obama Unmasked,* the international communist movement was joined by the American branch of the Roman Catholic Church in bringing Obama to power. That's why one chapter of *Comrade Obama Unmasked*, written by Michael Hichborn, was titled "The Catholic Candidate." This was like a "perfect storm" of powerful forces which came together on behalf of the "fundamental transformation" of the United States. But the election of Donald J. Trump as president was a powerful rejection of these forces, as he won more Catholics than his opponent, Hillary Clinton. What's more, his electoral success was predicated upon winning the workers who historically had voted for the Democratic Party.

**The Red Church**

One section of the Garrow book is a look back at Obama's Catholic connection in Chicago. It is interesting not only for historical reasons but because today the Roman Catholic Church on a global level is still firmly in the corner of the international Left and in fact can be considered part of the international communist movement. Still, Garrow only goes so far.

Doing the research and investigative work that the major U.S. media have all but abandoned, Michael Hichborn uncovered dramatic evidence of links between the highest levels of the Roman Catholic

Church and an international communist group known as the World Social Forum. The evidence suggests overt Marxist influence on the climate change movement that Pope Francis and his top advisers are now embracing.

Hichborn's report for the American Life League was a 76-page PowerPoint presentation complete with original source material and numerous photographs. It documents how Caritas Internationalis, the Vatican's top social justice organization, is actually "providing leadership" to the communist group. Hichborn stated, "This is a very serious problem. Given how intimately connected the World Social Forum (WSF) has been with the promotion of communism, abortion, and homosexuality since the very beginning, it's impossible to see how any Catholic can participate in it, or even speak positively about it, let alone have any involvement in its governance. But Caritas Internationalis does!"

These allegations can't be dismissed as anti-Catholic bigotry, since Hichborn is a traditional Catholic who has been working for years to expose Catholic funds and organizations that promote causes at variance with official Catholic teaching. The Hichborn report on the WSF includes eye-opening photographs from the group's events, featuring open displays of communist flags and banners as well as images of such personalities as Lenin, Castro and Mao.

Most of our media, of course, reported on the "death" of communism after the fall of the Berlin Wall.

But the Hichborn report notes, "There can be no mistaking the materialist and revolutionary (Communist) nature of the forum itself, which sets it in opposition to the Catholic Church." Hichborn said he delivered a copy of the report to the Vatican office known as Cor Unum, but that nothing came of it, and that one Vatican official concerned about the issue was relieved of his duties.

Hichborn identifies the other Catholic groups involved in the activities of the WSF as Pax Christi, Center of Concern, Sisters of Notre Dame de Namur, Catholic Relief Services and CIDSE, an international alliance of Catholic development agencies.

Our own independent review of the Hichborn report confirms the research into the links between Caritas Internationalis and the WSF. In fact, a document on the website affirms that "Caritas has been involved in the WSF since its beginnings. Caritas believes it's an opportunity to exchange ideas and to build the momentum towards real change."

After the Hichborn report was released, a conference at the Vatican was sponsored by Caritas Internationalis that featured Jeffrey Sachs, the Columbia University professor and Special Advisor to then-United Nations Secretary-General Ban Ki-Moon, and Gustavo Gutierrez, the father of Marxist-oriented Liberation Theology. Sachs had written an article for the Jesuit publication *America* attacking the "American idea" of life, liberty and the pursuit of happiness as narrow and selfish. He suggested that America's founding document is outmoded and incompatible with his idea of Catholic teaching about social justice.

Sachs is an advocate of global taxes to extract hundreds of billions of dollars from the American people in order to finance some form of world government. The climate change movement, based on dubious science, is the most popular current vehicle that Sachs and others are using to bring this about.

The World Social Forum held another international conference focusing on one aspect of the Sachs agenda: global taxes. The WSF announced the launch of the Global Alliance for Tax Justice, including a statement that "Our vision entails progressive redistributive taxation polices that fund the vital public services, end inequality and poverty, address climate change and lead to sustainable development."

At the Caritas conference, Pope Francis adviser Cardinal Oscar Rodríguez Maradiaga said that critics of the proposed papal document are advocates of an "ideology" that he concludes "is too tied to a capitalism that doesn't want to stop ruining the environment because they don't want to give up their profits."

Critics were concerned because of the pope's several statements indicating hostility to the system of capitalism and free markets that has brought prosperity to hundreds of millions of people.

This kind of Marxist rhetoric from a top Vatican adviser makes it appear as if the pope has aligned himself with an ideology that, despite the "collapse" of communism, is still very much alive.

The cordial Francis visit with Cuban dictator Raul Castro only added to the growing concern.

The title of the Caritas conference was, "One Human Family, Caring for Creation." But it appears that the "caring" part lies in replacing capitalism with structures of "global governance" that involve a massive transfer of political and economic power to international organizations like the United Nations.

As part of the push for "global governance," "cooperation" between European socialists and the Democratic Party has intensified significantly over the last several years. An event called the Global Progressive Forum was co-sponsored by the Socialist International, whose U.S. affiliate, the Democratic Socialists of America, includes long-time backers of Barack Obama, and the Party of European Socialists. Many of these groups came together at a "Global Progress Conference" in October, 2009, which featured President Barack Obama's pollster, Joel Benenson, as a speaker.

Significantly, it was announced in early August 2017 that Facebook CEO Mark Zuckerberg, a possible contender in the 2020 election, and his wife, Priscilla Chan, had hired Benenson to conduct "research" for the Chan Zuckerberg Initiative, the couple's $45 billion "philanthropic" project. [27] This kind of money and left-wing influence could make hedge fund billionaire George Soros look like a piker. [28]

Like other big companies such as Google, PayPal, and Twitter, Facebook has been accused of censoring conservatives on the Internet. [29]

**Civil War**

In his blockbuster film, "Civil War 2017," Trevor Loudon asks why the political left is so determined to destroy the Trump presidency. Matthew Vadum of the Capital Research Center responds that Trump "doesn't back down from a fight," unlike previous "squishy" Republicans. What's more, Trump has upended the "progressive coalition" by convincing millions of Democrats to abandon their union leaders and the Democratic Party.

Marxism in America is at a crossroads. And so are its adherents in the media, such as former Obama "Green Jobs Czar" and now CNN commentator Van Jones. He is smart enough to know that Trump has tapped into the anger and discontent of American workers. But at the same time, he is compelled to rally what remains of the progressive coalition against Trump. That is why he spoke at the "Women's March on Washington."

The job of uncovering the facts about the Obama communist network has fallen to groups like America's Survival, Inc., blogger Trevor Loudon, and those who contribute to our books, reports, conferences, and YouTube and Roku TV channels.

Loudon, who uncovered Jones' communist background, told me, "I began to investigate Van Jones after seeing several separate pieces of information. I first came across the name in the mid-1990s in a New Zealand socialist publication which had a small clip about Van Jones -- a Yale educated lawyer involved in STORM -- Standing Together to Organize a Revolutionary Movement. The name stuck."

While researching the far-left think Institute for Policy Studies, which Loudon considered the Obama administration's "ideas bank," Loudon found a piece by IPS staffer Chuck Collins recommending Van Jones for a top government job. A September 26, 2008 article, posted on the IPS website by Chuck Collins, offered 22 names they thought would make suitable appointments for an Obama administration. He included, "Van Jones, of the Ella Baker Center, to direct the Commerce Department's new 'green jobs initiative.'"

Remember that this was before the election.

"I researched Jones again at that point and found he was a fellow at the Center for American Progress," Loudon says, referring to the George Soros-funded entity.

Then a few days after the election he found a statement from former Weather Underground terrorist leader Mark Rudd, who was trying to ease fellow leftists' concerns at some of Obama's so-called "moderate" or "conservative" appointments, mostly in the economic realm. Rudd declared:

> Obama plays basketball. I'm not much of an athlete, barely know the game, but one thing I do know is that you have to be able to look like you're doing one thing but do another. That's why all these conservative appointments are important: the strategy is feint to the right, move left. Any other strategy invites sure defeat. It would be stupid to do otherwise in this environment.
>
> Look to the second level appointments. There's a whole govt. in waiting that [John] Podesta has at the [Soros-funded] Center for American Progress. They're mostly progressives, I'm told (except in military and foreign policy). Cheney was extremely effective at controlling policy by putting his people in at second-level positions.

Jones was appointed "Green Jobs Czar" in March 2009 at the White House Council on Environmental Quality. After his communist background came to light and he was fired, the Obama Administration refused to say how Jones was hired as the "Green Jobs Czar" and who recommended him. Glenn Beck later disclosed that it was Valerie Jarrett, Senior Advisor and Assistant to the President for Intergovernmental Affairs and Public Engagement, who claimed credit for the appointment during an appearance at a left-wing bloggers conference. Jarrett's late father-in-law, Vernon Jarrett, was an associate of Communist Party USA member Frank Marshall Davis.

Yet, the workers who used to be the cornerstone of the revolution have left the Democrats. They want economic and industrial development in traditional fossil fuel industries that the Democratic Party has been trying to bankrupt through the climate change hoax and green energy scams.

The January 21, 2017, Women's March on Washington was an indication of where the party is now finding money and support. The rally was financed by the abortion industry front known as Planned Parenthood and the environmentalist group called the Natural Resources Defense Council (NRDC).

The involvement of the NRDC is a reflection of the suicidal tendency that infects the Democratic Party. The NRDC's logo used to be a grizzly bear and later became a polar bear to shift the focus to climate change. This may appeal to liberal elites, but the workers who backed Trump would like to see some compassion for the workers losing their jobs to bad trade deals and climate change agreements that deindustrialize the U.S.

One organizer of the women's march, Rasmea Odeh, has subsequently been convicted of immigration fraud and ordered to be deported. Odeh, a member of the Marxist-Leninist Popular Front for the Liberation of Palestine (PFLP), perpetrated a 1969 supermarket bombing that killed two people. She had lied on immigration and naturalization forms about her conviction in Israel for the terror attack.

(The PFLP has issued a statement saluting the "anti-racist struggle in Charlottesville" and calling for "struggle against racism, fascism, Zionism and imperialism.") [30]

The so-called women's march featured communists like Angela Davis, who subsequently hosted the August 12 "Farewell to Rasmea Odeh" event in Chicago after she was ordered to be deported.[31]

Angela Davis started out with the Communist Party, became a lesbian, and is now a spokesman for animal rights. Along the way she was given the Lenin Peace Prize and praised Jim Jones, the religious cult leader who led his followers in a mass suicide and left his estate to the Communist Party.

In her speech, she called for "resistance" to Trump "on the ground, resistance in the classrooms, resistance on the job, resistance in our art and in our music."

She also thanked Obama for commuting the sentences of transgender traitor Bradley/Chelsea Manning and Puerto Rican terrorist Oscar Lopez Rivera. "We celebrate the impending release of Chelsea Manning," she said, "and Oscar Lopez Rivera. But we also say free Leonard Peltier. Free Mumia Abu-Jamal. Free Assata Shakur."

Peltier killed two FBI agents, while Abu-Jamal and Assata Shakur are convicted cop-killers. Shakur fled to Cuba and is living under the protection of that communist regime.

We argued back in 2013 that if the FBI wanted to find Assata Shakur/Joanne Chesimard, who was added to the "Most Wanted Terrorists List," it could begin by wiretapping Obama's friends, Bill Ayers and Bernardine Dohrn, and other members of the Weather Underground. The Weather Underground helped Chesimard -- a convicted cop-killer -- escape from a New Jersey prison in 1979 and flee to Cuba.

Clues as to how to find Chesimard were on display on November 13, 2010, when a memorial tribute was held for "Comrade" Marilyn Buck in New York City after she passed away. The sponsors highlighted a Chesimard recording in praise of Buck that had been smuggled out of Communist Cuba and played at the service. Former members of the Weather Underground and the Puerto Rican terrorist group, FALN, showed up to praise Buck as a great freedom fighter.

Bill Ayers and Bernardine Dohrn paid tribute to Buck in an announcement in the booklet distributed at her memorial service.

Chesimard is the most prominent communist terrorist still on the loose. But she is not the only one. Other fugitives on the FBI list include members of the May 19th Communist Organization. Joel Gilbert, director of the film, "Dreams from My Real Father," describes the

May 19th Communist Organization as "an above ground support group for the Weather Underground" that was based in New York City from 1978-1985. He says Obama was "likely" a member of the group during his time at Columbia University in the early 1980's. He notes that Obama, in his book, *Dreams from My Father*, describes attending several events in New York City (such as a Malcolm X movie screening) that are identical to documented May 19 events.

Elizabeth Ann Duke, a fugitive from justice considered "armed and dangerous" by the FBI, is yet another associate of Bill Ayers, notorious for her involvement with the May 19th Communist Organization and charged in the bombing of the U.S. Capitol, among other crimes.

Donna Joan Borup is another fugitive. In a radio broadcast about the case in 2013, the FBI noted that Borup, also considered armed and dangerous, became violent during a demonstration at JFK International Airport in Queens in September 1981 and tossed a caustic substance into the eyes of a Port Authority police officer who was on duty at the time. The officer was left partially blinded.

The FBI notes that "Borup was a member of the May 19th Communist Organization -- a Marxist-Leninist group advocating the armed revolution and overthrow of the United States government." It's likely that Bill Ayers and Bernardine Dohrn know the locations of these fugitives. They may even have told Obama.

**Communist Activity Increasing**

In the wake of the violence in Charlottesville in August, communist and anarchist groups have redoubled their efforts to take down President Trump.

The Democratic Socialists of America (DSA), which backed Obama's political career, issued a statement condemning "the white supremacist, racist, anti-Semitic terrorist attack on our comrades in the DSA, the ISO, IWW, Antifa and all others who joined forces in the streets of Charlottesville…" [32]

The ISO is the International Socialist Organization, while the IWW is the Industrial Workers of the World.

Under the headline, "Fight White Supremacy, Racism, and Fascism Everywhere!," the communist CCDS proclaimed:

> We condemn the white supremacist and neo-Nazi rally and violent assaults against anti-racist demonstrators which occurred in Charlottesville, Virginia, on August 12, 2017, resulting in the murder of one anti-racist protestor and severe injury to over a dozen more. We indict the Trump Administration for refusing to name and condemn the violence unleashed by the racist and neo-Nazi forces, while blaming both sides equally.

The Party for Socialism and Liberation said those on the Left must forge "steadfast unity in the streets -- as the heroes and martyrs of Charlottesville did…"

SocialistWorker.org said, "This Is the Time to Unite and Fight Far-Right Terror," even as it ran a series of articles marking the 100th anniversary of the Russian Revolution.

Another communist group, the Party of Communists USA, is rehabilitating the Soviet Union and offering it as a model:

> This year we celebrate the 100th anniversary of the socialist revolution in Russia. It was the first time that the working class anywhere in the world was able to seize and hold power. The revolution grew out of the conditions of imperialism and the First World War. Russia had been ruled by a tsar, or emperor, making it one of the most reactionary regimes in Europe…The great Afro-American activist Paul Robeson said about his trips to the Soviet Union, "I felt like a human being for the first time since I grew up. Here I am not a Negro but a human being."
>
> …The Soviet Constitution abolished racism and every man and woman were guaranteed the right to work, A 40-hour work week, social security, housing, food, education, and medical care were the law. Child labor was abolished; Homosexuality was decriminalized; and women

for the first time were granted the right to vote, hold office, and were paid the same wages as men.[33]

The group quotes Lenin as saying, "We, however, remain dialecticians and combat sophistry, not by a sweeping denial of the possibility of transformation in general, but by concretely analyzing a given phenomenon in the circumstances that surround it and in its development."

This is Marxist jargon, the kind that Barack Obama frequently used, that is meant to convey that the opportunity is at hand to create what Frank Marshall Davis and his comrades called a "Soviet America."

# End Notes

[1] See our ASI TV interview with Christopher Ferrara, "Russia, Fatima, and Bible Prophecy," posted on June 21, 2014.

[2] Kengor says, however, that the "CIA establishment" opposed naming the communists as being behind the plot.

[3] In his address before the Assembly of the Republic of Portugal in Lisbon, May 9, 1985, Reagan referred to Pope John Paul II as "the special man who came to Portugal a few years ago after a terrible attempt on his life. He came here to Fatima, the site of your great religious shrine, to fulfill his special devotion to Mary, to plead for forgiveness and compassion among men, to pray for peace and the recognition of human dignity throughout the world."

[4] "Robert Spencer: Pope Francis, Defender of Islam." See https://www.jihadwatch.org/2017/07/robert-spencer-pope-francis-defender-of-islam

[5] *The Hill* newspaper on August 21, 2017, reported that Obama's top aides "will huddle with him in the next several weeks to plan his fall schedule," and that "while his allies say he will play an active role in assisting the Democratic Party, much of the work will be out of public view."

[6] In a video, Dennis Prager asks why "communist" is so much less a term of revulsion than Nazi. One answer is that communism is "based on nice sounding theories" and Nazism isn't. See https://www.prageru.com/courses/history/why-isnt-communism-hated-nazism

[7] http://www.telegraph.co.uk/news/2017/08/09/crisis-venezuela-culmination-many-years-us-inaction-delusion/

[8] https://www.defense.gov/News/Article/Article/1281946/stratcom-commander-describes-challenges-of-21st-century-deterrence/source/GovDelivery/

[9] "Marulanda and the FARC for Beginners," Farc-epeace.org.

[10] http://www.cpusa.org/article/cpusa-contribution-to-world-communist-meet/

[11] The left-wing "fact-checking" website Snopes quotes Jason Kessler as saying that he was an Obama supporter and voted for him. He also reportedly says he was attracted to Occupy's "anti-

globalist" stance and attended an Occupy Charlottesville demonstration.

[12] *Investor's Business Daily* of December 11, 2015, said, "The panel had good cause to investigate. Communists hadn't just infiltrated Fisk as professors, but Johnson had readily hired them, including Giovanni 'Ross' Lomanitz, a known communist operative. Even after Lomanitz's communist loyalties were exposed, Johnson spoke out on his behalf. Johnson then hired and defended yet another communist, math professor Lee Lorch. Johnson initially refused to fire him, but relented under withering criticism."

[13] http://www.catholicamericanthinker.com/Marxist-Instigation.html

[14] https://vault.fbi.gov/cointel-pro/White%20Hate%20Groups

[15] https://www.fbi.gov/history/famous-cases/kkk-series

[16] http://www.workers.org/2017/08/15/cops-and-klan-hand-in-hand-lessons-of-charlottesville/

[17] https://www.centerforsecuritypolicy.org/wp-content/uploads/2016/11/Putins_Reset.pdf

[18] http://www.radionz.co.nz/national/programmes/ninetonoon/audio/201847460/the-making-of-barack-obama

[19] http://www.usasurvival.org/home/docs/weather_underground_bomb_factory.pdf

[20] http://www.usasurvival.org/home/docs/Declassified_docs.pdf

[21] Ibid.

[22] http://www.washingtontimes.com/news/2017/aug/1/russia-collusion-may-ensnare-john-mccain/

[23] http://www.washingtontimes.com/news/2017/jul/11/democrats-spread-false-russian-information-on-trum/

[24] Look under "Center for Investigative Journalism Special Reports" at www.aim.org

[25] http://www.cnn.com/2017/08/10/politics/kfile-sam-clovis-research/index.html

[26] http://leninandsharia.com/docs/Loudon-Alice-Palmer.pdf

[27] https://chanzuckerberg.com/

[28] Soros has led the way in transforming and destroying the

American system. See www.SorosFiles.com

[29] The book, *Islamic Jihad, Cultural Marxism and the Transformation of the West,* examines the role of Google as a new media "gatekeeper" that determines how people see the reality of the world. The author, William Mayer of PipeLineNews.org, examines how Google produces search engine results on the subject of Islamic terrorism that play down criminal activities of leading Jihadists. I was banned (temporarily) from the campus of the State University of New York at New Paltz by a feminist professor who used Google to search my name and then pass around derogatory information from the first source on the search engine page -- the Southern Poverty Law Center.

[30] http://pflp.ps/english/2017/08/15/pflp-salutes-anti-racist-struggle-in-charlottesville-calls-for-struggle-against-racism-fascism-zionism-and-imperialism/

[31] http://samidoun.net/2017/07/12-august-chicago-a-farewell-to-rasmea-odeh-with-angela-davis/

[32] http://www.dsausa.org/charlottesville

[33] http://www.partyofcommunistsusa.org/

Made in the USA
Monee, IL
23 September 2023